GW01281289

London Borough of Bromley

in old picture postcards volume 1

by
Muriel V. Searle

European Library – Zaltbommel/Netherlands

Acknowledgements
The author gratefully acknowledges those who have loaned pictures additional to her own collection, and especially: Rev. Tom Allen; Mr. Tony Banfield; Mr. Philip Daniell; ENBRO (Environment Bromley); HOBRA (Heart of Bromley Residents' Association); Lens of Sutton; Locomotive Club of Great Britain; Pamlin Prints Ltd.; Philip Lane Photography, in association with ENBRO; Mrs. Doris Pullen; Elsie Ransley; Rev. D. Redman; J. Salmon Ltd., Sevenoaks.

After several decades, it has proved difficult to contact copyright owners of some old pictures, but they are here acknowledged: P.A. Buchanan, Croydon; Gordon Chase Ltd.; J.N. Curwood Ltd.; Daniell Bros, Lewisham; Earle, Bromley; Field's Kent Series; Holdsworth, Kent House; Kingsway Series; T. Martin, Bromley; Photochrom; Scrivener & Co; W.J. Steed, Beckenham; Surrey Flying Services, Croydon; Valery, Beckenham.

Second edition: 1993

GB   ISBN 90 288 3331 5 / CIP

© 1985 European Library – Zaltbommel/Netherlands

No part of this book may be reproduced in any form, by print, photoprint, microfilm or any other means, without written permission from the publisher.

INTRODUCTION

During the two decades following the coming of railways, the average English town changed more than in the two previous centuries. This was specially true of places within about ten miles of London, which were first transformed into commercial towns, and then swallowed by the expanding city to become its outer suburbs.

Bromley was typical of this process; an ancient market town which eventually became a giant London Borough, though retaining areas of unspoilt countryside at its edges. Opened up by railways, it went through three main phases of modern development: the inexorable Victorian suburb-building boom, especially around Bromley North (vividly described by H.G. Wells as a semi-fictional Bromstead); the great housing growth of the 1920s and 1930s, spreading further out to engulf villages like Hayes, Orpington and West Wickham; and a lesser expansion after the Second World War. This book concentrates on the first two of these periods; a time that is now history, but believable history, peopled by characters of whom our grandparents still speak.

Recorded history began over a thousand years ago, with a charter of AD 862 wherein King Ethelbert mentioned land here. The name, too, is very old: literally Broom-lea, a lea (field or slope) covered by golden broom. It lasted until suburbanisation destroyed the shrubs, and Broom Day was once a major festival, when a huge procession wound through the town; the participants and spectators wore sprigs of broom on their clothes and hats.

Bromley's connection with the Bishops of Rochester was first mentioned in a will, and then in about AD 966 in a grant of property to the see by King Edgar. Thereafter, Bromley and the Bishops were synonymous. Their influence remains in many street names (Wendover, Murray, Glanville, Siward, Gundulph and Warner), and in Rochester Avenue. The final rebuilding of their ancient palace now forms the centrepiece of the Civic Centre.

In Domesday Book, 200 inhabitants were recorded, plus at least one mill. In 1205 came another landmark date, when Bishop Glanville asked permission of King John for a weekly market. For centuries it attracted people from miles around, coming first on foot or horseback, and then by train or bus; even now, Thursday is the principal weekday trading point, as thousands of shoppers instinctively follow tradition, though the market itself was moved in 1933 from the Square to a back street at Bromley North. Originally held on Tuesdays, the market was changed to Thursdays under Henry VI. Popular tradition believed that if no stall was set up on any Thursday, Bromley Market would forfeit its right to exist; and that if Christmas Day fell on a Thursday, at least one stall must trade to uphold this historic right.

In 1327 local people became ratepayers, after Bishop Hamo De Hythe imposed a levy on residents of manor lands for repairing his crumbling church.

Bromley College, the largest and loveliest historic possession, was founded in 1666 after Bishop Warner left the then enormous sum of £8,000 for its foundation. Hearsay attributes it, without proof, to Wren. It contains exquisite cloisters and a charming chapel, rarely open to the public. A famous early movie, 'The Rosary', is said to have been filmed there.

Modern Bromley began to develop after 1792, when the surgeon James Scott grew in reputation. So famous was he for joint and hip treatment, and so sensational his cures, that wealthy patients built fine houses (notably on Bromley Common) to be near him, starting a small property boom. 'Scott's Coaches' ferried others from London. Scott reputedly once made £10,000 a year, when £50 was an average wage.

Riches contrasted with poverty, however, as the 'Hungry Forties' struck. Shops failed and closed, traders moved out, and mobs looted bread from a Market Square bakery. Between the 1841 and 1851 censuses, the population actually declined.

But in the 1850s a return to prosperity was heralded by a salute of guns, fired from the top of Martin's Hill to welcome the first train from Shortlands station, which temporarily acted as the stop for Bromley, until Bromley South was opened. Commuterdom was born, enabling men to work in London but live near the country. Innumerable roads of all-alike villas sprouted to house this new generation, and in only a decade the population doubled. Bromley North opened in 1878, and another wave of suburb-building engulfed the meadows and destroyed the remaining broom. Nearby, in South Street, the tiny cottage where H.G. Wells attended dame-school still exists, and a blue plaque on Allders' store marks the site of his birthplace. His father, Joseph, was a shopkeeper and professional cricketer, regularly playing on the White Hart Field (now Queen's Gardens), where notable 'swipes' with the bat were recorded.

The miserable little market house looked suddenly unsuitable for a growing town, until in 1863 Coles Child built a Gothic Town Hall in its place: solid, stolid and worthy rather than inspired. It became a cultural and municipal centre, noted for a superb sprung dance floor. Dancing, with the 'flicks' (cinema), reached a peak of popularity in the 1920s and 1930s; Bromley had other fine ballrooms, at the White Hart and where the Odeon now stands. At the Gaumont super-cinema elaborate stage shows were given, including the now legendary 'Eight Piano Symphony'. The Gaumont has been adapted as Debenhams' department store, but most of its original exterior is recognisable.

The Second World War drew a firm line between the happy Thirties and the birth of modern history, and obliterated some landmarks for ever. In April 1941 seven churches were blitzed in one night; the historic Parish Church became an inferno, and its tower a huge flaming chimney; in the present chancel one window shows this terrifying scene, with the new church rising from the old.

What war did not destroy, modernity has attacked with concrete and glass instead of with bombs. So much that was lovely has gone, or been unhappily altered. In this collection we record both these categories, and sigh for the Bromley that has vanished.

1. The soul of Bromley lost lingers vividly in this scene of 1913 in the Market Square. In the centre is the Victorian Town Hall, whose demolition reduced the scale of the whole area, and around which were many stalls. Lying low at the left is the heavy portico of Skilton's butchery, outside which is a rattling open topped bus; otherwise the traffic is limited mainly to bicycles. Just round the right-hand corner was the small shop where H.G. Wells was born; a few yards away, out of the picture at extreme right, was The Little Shop; a tiny old wooden shack selling mainly sweets, where the future author spent his Saturday pocket money. It was demolished a few years ago, and in the rubble the writer's father recognised an historic holy water stoup, presumably discarded by the adjoining Parish Church; the find was immediately reported at the present church.

2. This postcard is of uncertain date, but shows the lower High Street as it looked between the 1930s and 1950s. Much has changed since. The ornate lamp standards are gone, and the pretty rustic fencing. Only one shop (Ayling's) remains in the same ownership on the right-hand Broadway terrace. Big chain stores in severe modern buildings continue up the street, with The Mall shopping precinct. The Wesleyan Church with tower, in pale grey stone, was demolished for more shops. Opposite it is seen the beautiful old Library, now replaced by the towering Churchill Theatre and Library block. At left is part of the Gaumont Cinema, whose shell now houses a department store; it had a large ballroom over the front. Next door a tall Victorian house was occupied by three doctors – Dysart, Walker and Wishart – and had its own dispensary for making up the more common medicines.

3. Almost nothing remains of the left side of the High Street as seen in this view postmarked 1909. At that period a forge still existed. One gown shop on the other side boasted one of the earliest revolving doors in the district. The turreted Town Hall was replaced by today's mock-Tudor Square, but even more interesting is the tall chimney just visible to its left, part of the long forgotten Bromley Electric Light Works. When demolished in the 1920s or 1930s, on a Sunday morning, crowds jammed the street to watch the fun. The old Electric Light Works' very existence was little known until the author, told about it by her father, tipped off a local conservation group; they identified substantial buildings hidden away, and began fighting for their survival.

4. Cabs and carts throng the Victorian streets. The huge lantern long ago vanished, but in compensation we have the restoration to the far side of the Square of Bromley's old town pump, handsomely repainted. For years it was neglected and relegated to a corner in Church House Gardens, under a hedge, but it was removed in 1985 for this refurbishment. The Royal Bell (left) replaced a low-slung coaching inn whose outer character was not unlike the surviving Swan and Mitre. As late as 1880 coaches with passengers sitting on top, behind a four-in-hand, rattled past this corner. The last Hansom cabs lingered into the 1920s, when nostalgic farewell rides were taken by Bromley people.

5. Town Hall Buildings typify the stately, fancifully ornamented style of the late Victorian and early 20th century periods, and also the predominance of private businesses, whereas today Bromley is dominated by chain stores. They include Covell & Harris, the corner butchers, catering mainly for 'the more influential families of the neighbourhood'. Shops in this area often employed floor-walkers; solemn men in black whose purpose was to greet valued customers with great politeness, escort the ladies to chairs at the counters, and enquire as they left if Madam was satisfied. There was even a specialist in pet cat and dog photography, a saddler and harness maker, and an ice merchant, whose directory entry carried the By Appointment crest of the Imperial Family of France.

6. This now lost Town Hall was unusual in being made entirely by workers employed by the Lord of the Manor, Coles Child, instead of by a contractor, and was dominated by an ornate tower. It included a police station and cells, auction rooms, and a Literary Institute, above which was the grand 60-foot-long main hall. It was truly a town hall: a hall for the town, rather than administrative offices. During the Great War the local Food Office was set up, dealing with rationing and distribution. Here the staff pose at the main door in about 1915, including Mr. W. Brooks, the manager, and Nellie Jessop (centre), later the writer's mother. Among regular wartime callers was a Miss Wells, an aunt of H.G. Wells, though his branch of the family had long since left Bromley.

7. Virtually everything in this historic picture has now gone: the handsome library (here described as new); the pretty cottages which survived until recently, one as an old jeweller's shop; and the block including the Grand Hall, later called the New Theatre until destroyed by fire. This library was a very mellow and comfortable building. Records of staff salaries reveal that in 1913 the Head Librarian's pay was increased by £10 a year, and that for the Assistant Librarian by £5; scarcely ten modern pence a week. Sunday opening plans were then under discussion, involving the National Amalgamated Union of Shop Assistants, Warehousemen and Clerks and also, rather oddly, the United Operative Plumbers' Association. Behind this library was Bromley's famous floral clock, composed entirely of tiny plants.

8. Aberdeen Buildings today survive as the High Street's most precious possession, ornately dated 1887. They are uniquely designed in the French Empire manner, presumably in tribute to the French Imperial Family who lived in exile at Camden Place, Chislehurst; the Empress Eugenie often drove in by carriage to patronise local shops or attend events. To the right a fraction of the Wesleyan Church is seen; beyond, an assortment of cottages and shops whose sites are mostly now occupied by chain stores like Marks & Spencer or Littlewoods, banks, and other modern shops. The trees long ago vanished in favour of Bromley's burgeoning commerce.

9. In December 1772 John Wesley came preaching to embryonic Widmore, and again in the following October. He can hardly have visualised such developments as this stately Wesleyan Church in Bromley High Street, opened in 1876. In soft grey stone (unusual in this mainly brick built town) it lay back behind fine trees, until they were felled and its courtyard shrunk for road widening. After wartime damage and repair, the church closed after the 1964 Watch Night service, and its valuable site is now but a very plain office and shop block. It was replaced by a modern church complex behind the old site, in Holwood Road, into which some fragments were incorporated. This picture also shows how old houses (right) were adapted into shops as Bromley's commerce grew, by utilising their former front forecourts.

10. 'Bromley, of course,' is the answer when, in Jane Austen's 'Pride and Prejudice', a character asks where coach horses will be changed. The Bell and White Hart serviced numberless daily coaches and carriages travelling from London to regal Tunbridge Wells, or to Hastings. In its heyday the White Hart could take about a hundred horses, and the Bell about eighty. The present gracious Bell building replaced a 17th century coaching inn. The prefix Royal (the Royal Bell) came from its handling of royal carriages in the 19th century; when royalty arrived, the ostlers and grooms were required to don a special scarlet livery. A few yards away stood for many years the small Walter Tarry tailoring shop; its intricately carved frontage is now in the Museum of London.

11. The Broadway as few people today can even imagine it, innocent of the eternal buses, lorries and cars of a busy main road towards London. The old Kentish character lingers in shops that vanished long ago, except for one on the background block. The right-hand side is still countrified, where Debenham's and Waring & Gillow's giant stores now stand, along with other modern shops. The road is poorly made, though soon to be paved with thousands of wood blocks; these in turn were tarred over, lasting into the 1950s. Even post-war, a few private businesses lingered: Kennedy's fishmongery with its giant propeller fans and fanciful advertisements for 'Bromley Bay Crabs', Last's secondhand book cellar, and even an 'Uncle's' (pawnbroker).

12. Skilton's butchery was among Bromley's most impressive older shops, dominating the west side of the Market Square. Its heavy marble pillars carried a canopy out almost to the kerb, enabling well-off customers to drive up by carriage or early motor car and descend without exposure to the weather. Its interior is remembered as being thickly scattered with sawdust, and whole sheep and cows could be seen hanging from traditional butchers' hooks; in season, dozens of rabbits were hung up, complete with fur. Next door stood Isard's hardware shop, stocking fuels and household goods; it, too, had a distinctive aroma; of wood, paper, leather, paint and paraffin. It suffered three disastrous fires among its highly flammable stock. Both these historic buildings were demolished for a modern supermarket.

13. A now little known royal visit to Bromley, when in November 1920 the Duke of York (later to become King George VI) came to the ex-Servicemens' Club, with whose Executive he is pictured here. The founder and first Chairman of Bromley British Legion — the author's grandfather — stands immediately behind the Duke (right) in this group posed after a formal royal inspection of the Club. At the Central Hall, which was afterwards destroyed by bombing during the 1940s, the Duke opened a fair staged in aid of the Star And Garter Fund. This ceremony was attended by many local nurses in uniform, and the hall was heavily decorated with flags. Leaving the Central Hall, the Duke of York was saluted by a guard of honour of the Bromley scouts.

14. Every butcher commissioned a trade-photograph, used in local directories and Christmas advertisements, or sold as a card, with row on row of rabbits and poultry hung outside; there was precious little traffic then to raise contaminating dust. Banks' of Aberdeen Buildings cashed in on 'those augmentations of population and trade' as this old country town moved towards suburbdom. The shop delivered twice daily round Bromley and out to Elmers End, Chislehurst, Orpington and beyond. Tradesmen were counted 'respectable': below the gentry but above the artisan class, taking prominent parts in local affairs. For example, Harris the optician was also an astronomer, with his own observatory at Keston, while Head's made their own cutlery, still occasionally found surviving today.

15. 'Alexander Tosland, Upholsterer and Art Furnisher' in the High Street, added whimsical Moorish embellishments to his frontage, complementing the filigree of his lace curtains. 'In this art-loving age such an establishment as Mr Tosland's is a necessity,' commented one trade directory. His clientele was therefore mainly the wealthy, when Bromley was noted for its many country seats and large aristocratic households. For them also operated the Court dressmaking business named Cakebread's, occupying upstairs rooms close to the Star and Garter; Miss Cakebread read the Bible aloud as her child apprentices worked on elaborate tucks and pleats. For this a 13-year-old girl received one shilling (5p) a week; any request for a rise was refused on the grounds that 'we are teaching you a trade'.

Central Hall, Bromley.

16. Of the churches and chapels lost during the Blitz, one of the saddest losses was the Central Hall (Methodist); not only for religious reasons but also because it had been a centre of good music. Its three-level platforms could accommodate large numbers of performers, and Sunday afternoons in particular were a marvellous combination of music and worship. The Hall had its own ensemble, the Central Hall Orchestra, which accompanied choirs and visiting soloists in large scale anthems and oratorios. One regular visitor was the pianist W.H. Jude, who was believed to have given up a lucrative concert career to perform and write sacred music. The site is now occupied by an office block, but the smaller Sunday School hall survives at the rear.

PARISH CHURCH, BROMLEY.

17. The town motto of pre-London-Borough Bromley, 'Dum Cresco Spero' ('While I grow I Hope') in this 1905 card sums up the vicissitudes of its ever changing church: pulled down, rebuilt, demolished again, rebuilt again. During the 1941 blitz inferno the tower shown here became a huge chimney, flames shooting from the top, and the bells crashed down in a molten mass. But in 1951 they rang again, recast from the old metal and re-hung in the restored tower. In the present ringing room is a miniature bell frame showing how a church bell is hung and rung. This little bell, number sixteen, was rescued intact: not a full model but one of a set of old handbells. It was rigged up to demonstrate the technique to new ringers, children, and visitors such as those allowed up the tower to see the magnificent view from the top, on just one day a year during the big open day and fair held at Petertide.

18. Only the skilfully restored tower survives from Bromley's pre-blitz parish church. Everything else was splintered into fragments in 1941. The handsome replacement nave is set back behind the tower instead of as in this picture of the old church; it includes a Children's Chapel with a memorial window to Hazel Kissick, the schoolgirl who died that night in the church whilst firewatching. One of the few things saved was the tombstone of 'Tetty', Dr. Johnson's wife; hence the naming of a new adjoining byroad as Tetty Way. Few Bromleians now realise that parts of their lost church can be seen only yards away: much of the rubble was heaped up below the terraces in Church House Gardens to form a giant rockery. Evidence is fading with the years, but a close look still identifies incised work and the outlines of pillar and arch stones on some of the boulders.

19. Bromley Congregational Church was another blitz victim, whose cluttered interior is shown in about 1919. During the First World War 'The Cong' played its part 'In defence of Righteousness, Liberty and Truth'. Belgian refugees were taken in by church people and the Dence family house in Valley Road was made over to the church and furnished for the 36 newcomers by members. Christmas gifts went to Bromley men fighting at the Front, and they received a monthly newsletter and a copy of the 'Church Record'. The Soldiers' Club was legendary for its entertainment for troops billeted locally, who were detailed to see lady musicians and entertainers safely home after their performances. 'They came in thousands for a meal, a smoke, a wash, games, reading, conversation, music and letter writing,' a Congregational report recorded.

20. Suburban Bromley in the making: terraces appear where there were recently open fields in this postcard of the early 1930s. The villa marked with a cross was the estate show-house: it cost just over £700. The road is still roughly surfaced, and woodlands survive in the background. Part of this avenue was built over an ancient pond. Two disasters later hit Queen Anne Avenue. In the 1940s blitz an air-raid wardens' post was bombed, killing several people while on duty – the huge crater could have held a bus – which is recalled by a plaque honouring 'lives lost in loyal service and devotion to duty', and in a memorial shrubbery. In 1968 a major flood engulfed the whole road, with water up to three feet deep *inside* some houses.

21. Ruby Verrell's 'Dainty Blossoms' were an immensely popular local dancing troupe, the best pupils of her ballet school. They worked between the world wars, and up to about the 1960s. The 'Dainty Blossoms' massed displays were almost legendary, spectacular for the sheer numbers of children taking part in folk, character and ballet numbers. Ruby Verrell herself, when young, was noted for her beautiful hair, forming masses of intricate ringlets or crimped to fall far down her back. In those days, picture postcards of stage, film and music-hall stars were circulated in thousands. Even regional artists received this treatment, at more local level, as in this undated example.

22. This thatched bandstand in the Library Gardens was most unusual; in years of travel, the author has never seen another. It stood near the middle of the small upper pond, surrounded by water and accessible only by a picturesque humped wooden bridge. The whole main construction was also of timber, in the rustic style. A countryman familiar with the thatcher's art gave it the highest accolade he knew, in the 1930s: 'Ee be a noice bit o' thatch.' Facing it, a curved arena of gravelled shallow steps seated hundreds of listeners on green metal chairs. Inevitably the new post-war vandalism saw it as an arson target. It was soon re-thatched, only to flame again in a final spectacular blaze. The remains were removed, and replaced by a plain concrete stage on the other side of the water.

23. Hidden behind The Broadway shops today are some original mews. Before motor vehicles, shopkeepers kept their horses and carts there, with hay in the loft above. The Singer Sewing Machine shop ran Jane I and Jane II, which the manager drove around delivering heavy iron treadle machines, and collecting payments on the 'never-never': a colloquialism for hire-purchase. Behind Singer's counter was the shop parlour: a lovely Victorian name for a stockroom and office. At the rear (now built over to extend a stationery shop) was a garden massed with old fashioned flowers. In the days of horse traffic, garden-proud traders went onto the High Street with buckets and spades whenever manure was wanted. This part of the High Street was surfaced by thousands of wooden blocks until about 1950; when removed, many were sold as firewood.

24. Three superb lamps swing above a Broadway business, to increase the otherwise poor street lighting of the period; another of several high-class drapers and milliners. The three 'triple burner lamps' were among the marvels of Bromley. Ladies were served with corsets for constricting their voluptuous figures, heavily whaleboned and placketed, together with ribbons, gloves, and the fashionable knick-knacks dismissed by the jealous lower classes as 'fripperies'. This shop stood on the Broadway, where the lower High Street opened out into newer buildings: literally a broad-way, after the narrow older Square area.

25. No TV existed during the Great War to show people at home what 'the boys' were enduring at the Front: the mud, the cold, the fighting, the primitive trenches. To help people understand, Bromley staged a Gun Day or Trench Day, when mock-ups were made behind the Municipal Buildings or in the Square. This dim but rare postcard shows a Gun Day installation, and also the portable lights for floodlighting the trenches at night. It was probably taken in about 1915 or 1916.

26. Scouts take a break from building their own Third Bromley group headquarters in Glanville Road, in the late 1920s or early 1930s; very much a do-it-yourself job. Local Scouting, in the First Bromley troop, grew out of two early school groups, and in 1909 was followed by a Second Bromley initially composed of boys on holiday from public schools. In February 1912 the committee of the Bromley Boy Scouts' Local Association first met. By the great suburban housing boom period, in 1933, over eight hundred Scouts were recorded in Bromley. In 1925 they staged a monster Gala Day in the Palace grounds, including a march-past of sixteen troops before Major Baden-Powell.

27. Bromley Market Square lives in local lore for the ferocity of the fires which have periodically wrecked its businesses. Until modern times, the combination of flammable goods and fuels, hay and fodder, and primitive brigade equipment was always potentially lethal. Apart from three big blazes at Isard's premises in 1828, 1882 and 1921, there was this scene photographed in about 1909, watched by huge crowds swathed in a dense fog of smoke. Old residents can still describe how volunteers led working horses from the stables during one major Square fire, braving falling beams and clouds of sparks; and how one terrified animal broke free and galloped back inside. Finally came the 'Great Fire of Bromley', in February 1968 when Harrison Gibson's huge furnishing shop, lower down the High Street, became for the second time a vast inferno.

28. One of the most vital battles to preserve Bromley's green heritage was won in 1985, when a plan to enclose part of Martins Hill for a commercial ski-slope was defeated. It was not the first threat: previously planners have tried to build a road across the lower Hop Field (once the nearest to London), and to take it for housing. As a Victorian protester wrote: 'May never innovating hand deprive the town of Martins Hill.' This attractive hilltop lodge of 1887 is here seen before erection of the war memorial, on a card mailed during the Great War. The right-hand fountain seems to have been moved downhill to Queens Mead, itself bought to celebrate Victoria's Jubilee. Martins Hill has occasionally been a natural grandstand for major firework displays, the setpieces being on one slope and the spectators on the other.

29. From the pioneer days of radio comes this beautiful radio cabinet entirely hand-made in Bromley, including the internal works, by the author's father Noel Searle, in 1933; he was the first customer at Bromley's first radio shop. The all-electric receiver and gramophone and their personally designed and crafted cabinet were publicised in wireless magazines of the period, as pointing towards new developments. The speakers were behind the small front door and over the desk section. The whole could be switched on without opening it up; a big improvement on shop-made models. Painstaking craftsmanship like this, when enthusiasts built every part themselves, vanished once mass production began.

30. Ballroom dancing reached its zenith in the 1920s and 1930s. Bromley had both professional and semi-professional bands. The famous Jack Payne (nicknamed 'Jack's Back' because he rarely faced his audience) regularly appeared here. Local groups included the Premier Dance Orchestra, Robson Four, Elraes Dance Band, and Lancaster-Reeves Dance Orchestra. Even factory workers formed their own dance bands, like this one based at the Kolster Brandes works at Sidcup, just outside the present Borough, but active throughout Bromley area. The instrumental composition was very different from today, as this postcard dated February 1930 reveals, generally including violin, piano and banjo, plus the more usual saxophone, percussion, clarinet and trumpet or trombone.

31. In the schools of yesteryear, every boy in some classes was given a small school-issue violin, such as a 'Maidstone', which only cost about five shillings (25p). Most never became musicians, but each group usually produced at least one with more talent than the others. In this picture is the author's father Noel Searle (extreme right of third row up); one of those who did make the grade, as a film and theatre violinist and as leader of four Bromley dance bands. This Aylesbury Road School class was taught by a Mr. Vallance (centre group at right), a second violinist at the Penge Empire, earning the union rate of £1 a night. Mr. Lewis, headmaster, sits in the centre.

COUNTY SCHOOL FOR BOYS, HAYES LANE, BROMLEY, KENT

32. Bromley County School For Boys was opened in 1910 under the headmastership of Reginald Airy. This picture, from an aircraft probably flying out of the then important Croydon Aerodrome, shows the main buildings almost alone in open countryside; there is no sign of the suburban houses later added along the road, which is totally devoid of traffic. This school was given a magnificent hall with a very ornate ceiling, which became a home for Bromley Symphony Orchestra. Most of their concerts between the 1940s and 1970s were given there, sometimes under the great conductor Sir Adrian Boult. A lifelong friend of the orchestra's leading figures, the Whyte sisters of Ripley, he conducted at least one concert each season and in 1964 made a unique record with the orchestra, including Hindemith's then rarely played 'Trauermusik'.

Bromley County Girls' School Form Room.

33. This picture shows children in one of the original classrooms of the then Bromley County School For Girls, in 1921. They wear the navy gymn-slip which was standard in schools until after the Second World War. This consisted of a simple square-necked yoke and several very wide falling pleats, belted with a webbing girdle (knotted like a man's tie) in the colour of the girl's school house. Houses were named after famous Kentishmen like Darwin, Pitt, Sidney, Wolfe and Chaucer. Strangely, gymn-slips were not worn in the gymnasium, where girls changed into navy shorts and white singlets. This school opened in 1905 and has since been continually enlarged.

Bromley County Girls' School Gardens.

34. This was the full extent of the Girls' County School in Nightingale Lane as it looked in 1921, before the modern extensions making it a sprawling complex. The school garden is shown here, where girls learned correct methods of weeding, planting, raising seeds and producing their own vegetables. In May 1955 this school celebrated its jubilee with a service in the then new Parish Church. The two lessons were read by the headmistress and the chairman of governors.

BROMLEY COUNTY SCHOOL FOR GIRLS. *Gordon Chase, Ltd.*

35. In 1921 this was the full frontage of the Girls' County School, set between Bromley and Bickley with playing fields running down to the railway. Next door was the gasworks, whose smells drifted across the fields during hockey and cricket matches. Gas fumes when imbibed out of doors were alleged by some mothers actually to be 'good for you', making this a healthy school. Massed school photographs were periodically taken, and the 1948 group is now in the Public Library's local history collection. It was taken by an ingenious special camera panning slowly across the entire school, banked up on chairs and forms in a giant semi-circle; the result came out as a straight line about twenty inches wide, to be framed and hung in pupils' homes.

36. Church House, set next to the Parish Church, is now but a gracious memory and a few fading photographs. Only the terracotta-coloured terrace commanding views towards Keston and Biggin Hill is left of the creeper-covered mansion and its lavish greenhouses. The entrance drive and lawn also survive, inside the Church Road gates. This impeccable oval shaped lawn was long regarded as the finest piece of grass in Bromley; it was not even desecrated by a 'Keep off the grass' sign, but nobody dreamed of stepping on it. A tiny goldfish pond surrounded by somewhat overgrown shrubs, on the open space of the terrace, now marks the site of this lost house. This picture dates from the early twenties.

Bromley South Station. *Bromley.*

37. Bromley South as present commuters know it bears little relation to this leisured scene, where the local bobby can stand and stare; today traffic is eternally rushing past, on one of the busiest main roads out of London. Bromley's biggest railway disaster happened in the late 19th century at the Ivy Bridge, not far beyond the ends of the Down platforms, which collapsed onto a hut full of men having breakfast. They had been brought in after half the bridge suddenly fell, to make safe the other half. Ivy Bridge had lived up to its name, the festoons of growth hiding dangerously widening cracks until the whole bridge collapsed. Even now, there are weight and speed restrictions over the bridge which replaced it.

38. A group of early poppy-sellers working for the Armistice Day collections. One lady is pinning a November poppy for the founder-chairman of Bromley British Legion. In the background, Bromley South station, with its advertisements for the new Southern Electric trains, reminds us how much the locality changed when railways came. To quote a Bromley journal, way back in 1869: *It was... considered one of the most ridiculous and extravagantly insane notions that ever entered the mind of mortal man, to suppose that a coach would travel without any horses; but now the wonder is to see a coach* with *horses.* Now, in the 1920s, had come another wonder: trains without locomotives. Near here was a railway type nameboard not fixed to any station: the sign of Ravensbourne Halt, this being the name of a sweet shop.

39. A very leisured Bromley South station in the 1920s, where milkchurns wait for a train, before suburban roads destroyed most of the dairying country around the town. A secondary sign reading 'South' has been hung below the 'Bromley' name board, to differentiate it from the newer Bromley North. Steam trains were seen here into the 1960s, because the war interrupted electrification, which ended at Gillingham; thus Ramsgate, Dover and Canterbury services were still steam hauled by such marvellous classes as the *Schools, Merchant Navy* and *King Arthur*. Mothers often took children up to the engine as it stood waiting, to thank the driver for a safe journey; sadly, full electrification killed the courtesy as well as the romance of steam.

40. The Jovials Concert Party, active around Bromley in the 1920s. Local concert parties, often drawn from one family, were immensely popular, performing in church halls and the Drill Hall; the latter was the foremost entertainment centre of the town, modest though it looks today in decline, staging major civic banquets as well as the Police Minstrels or Christmas parties given by big landowners for their staffs. A concert party performed a variety show made of various 'turns' such as piano solos, banjo playing, poetry, recitations, acrobatics, comedy and melodrama, and simple sketches. Many emphasised their local status by appearing under their own surnames: another good example were the Corrick Family Entertainers, again performing around Bromley and south-east London.

41. The top of Martins Hill seen soon after erection of the War Memorial, in the early Twenties. To the left is a tall house, probably 'Stoberry', whose place is occupied by the modern St. Paul's Square; its gardens were in spring full of wild snowdrops. Behind this was the rambling Victorian vicarage, set in big grounds, and also a superb Queen Anne or Georgian house in red brick, with a gas lamp outside; beside this was a row of tiny cottages. All these perished either in the wartime blitz by bombs, or in the peacetime blitz by builders. The church tower seen here was skilfully rebuilt after the bombing, being the only fragment spared from the historic Parish Church.

42. A peacetime school playground becomes a wartime mock battleground. The scene is a Bromley school (possibly Raglan Road) in about 1915, where under the sharp eye of a uniformed officer, first-aid training is being carried out. Some men are working with stretcher poles while others attend to the prostrate 'victims'. Though Bromley has a fine hilltop war memorial, another one erected to the dead of the First World War was destroyed in the bombing of the next war, being set inside the old Parish Church. It had described men like these as 'fighting for God, and Right, and Liberty', and added that in those causes they had suffered 'the noblest death a man may die'.

16516 OLD LODGE, BECKENHAM LANE.   BROMLEY.

43. Beckenham Lane, where this delightful old long-lost lodge once stood, is also known locally as Swan Hill, after the historic Swan And Mitre at the top. It is steep and winding. One old resident has told the author how she saw a cart horse with a heavy load of coal collapse in the shafts and fall on the road near this corner; and how he was beaten until he dragged himself up and staggered on. Within living memory most of the land behind this cottage was thickly forested, known unofficially as Highland Road Woods after that then lonely thoroughfare, where girls were afraid to walk alone at night. Their morale was not improved by brothers who pointed out a sinister turreted corner house alleged to be haunted. Folklore holds that early 20th century estate agents lowered its price because this legend frightened off buyers.

SHORTLANDS ROAD AND CHURCH ROAD.

44. In 1869 a local paper observed: *In this fashionable locality large houses are constantly springing up, and as a consequence the roads get worn and out of repair, and their present state is being much complained of.* Gentility was the keynote of developing Shortlands, as one is reminded when walking around the St. Mary's area today, where older properties range from tall town houses with servants' rooms in the attics, to mansions big enough to become residential homes or blocks of flats. In this view Church Road meets Shortlands Road, where traffic now incessantly sprints towards Beckenham. Though Church Road itself is quiet, it is still hardly the place to sit and meditate on a public bench set in the middle of the road, like this one shown in a postcard dated 1915.

45. It seems impossible now that the world could ever have looked as undeveloped as this wilderness, where Farnaby Road and its companion avenues now stand. This picture dates from the early to mid-1920s, just before the main onrush of development for housing began, especially in the wake of Southern Railway suburban electrification, making it easier and quicker than ever before to live in a desirable suburb and work in town. Those houses are now matured, over half a century old; when this scene was recorded, they were only a plan lying on some speculative developer's desk.

PREMISES AT HIGH STREET, BROMLEY.

46. Weeks' shop was every inch the emporium of old, selling everything and anything to everybody: lawnmowers, spades, iron mangles, brass and copper ware, lampshades and oil lamps, locks, bolts and hardware. They were always ahead of modern development: 'In view of the probable introduction of electric lighting into the town, the firm have added to their practice as fitters of electric bells and burglar alarms... the business of electric lighting engineers, and are now prepared to fit up installations,' was their early 20th century boast. In the 1930s they were quick to offer a 'wonder refrigerator' on hire-purchase for ten shillings (50p) deposit, or just over £19 cash. Weeks' even advertised themselves as 'bell hangers'.

47. A postcard with an adventurous history. It was bought in Bromley in the early 1930s, and was next discovered some years later and three thousand miles away — in America! Recognising the view from Martins Hill, the finder posted it back to a relative in Bromley, where it has been treasured ever since. Even now Martins Hill is tranquil, commanding the same view over three counties (Kent, Surrey and London), and the valley here shown is still thick with trees as well as moderately developed for housing. In the Thirties it was enriched by the distant Crystal Palace on Sydenham Hill, whose thousands of glass panes glittered like a giant mirror in the afternoon sun.

LYCH GATE ST MARY'S CHURCH SHORTLANDS

48. The lych-gate of old St. Mary The Virgin looked older than it really was, like the entrance to an ancient country church. Even now the surrounding roads, though suburbanised, are treelined, dignified and quiet. St. Mary's attracted a well-to-do congregation as Shortlands became a gentlemen's retreat. Among distinguished residents of nearby Church Road was the famous electrical pioneer Alexander Muirhead, whose achievements included a means of recording the human heart-beat, predating today's ECG machines. After this he returned to precision electronic instruments and submarine cables. A large factory near Elmers End still bears the name of Muirhead, and there is a blue commemorative plaque on his old home.

49. The Premier Dance Orchestra plays outdoors on Queens Mead during August Bank Holiday of 1925, making themselves heard by good musicianship rather than microphones. The stage is a few rough planks. The Mead was used much more than it is now for public events, such as the monster outdoor party for schoolchildren on Edward VII's coronation. Travelling funfairs pitched there, on the railway side, into the 1950s, when they were banished on account of the damage done to the field by the rides and sideshows: though in reality nature always quickly repaired it. The River Ravensbourne was here a pretty country stream, until harshly canalised for flood prevention; before that, the entire Mead became a muddy lake after any heavy storm.

50. St. Mary's Shortlands, destroyed forty years ago, lives in this pre-war picture. The altar and reredos confirm that it was unusually 'High' for its time, following the fashionable Oxford Movement when most others opposed ceremonial. In 1884 the mixed choir was replaced by men and boys in the cathedral manner, later robed in full cassocks and surplices: almost Popish in diehard 19th century Bromley. St. Mary's also boldly adopted the controversial new 'Hymns Ancient & Modern'. Next to nothing remained of this richly decorated interior after the bombings of 1941 and 1944.

51. An elaborate carved font dominates this interior view of the now destroyed St. Mary the Virgin, Shortlands; part of the organ is also visible. Unhappily, little was saved from the bomb wreckage of 1944, except for the High and Lady altars, a bookcase, brass crosses and a lectern, and a few items of furniture. From its hilltop St. Mary's looked down on the fields supposed to be one possible explanation of the placename. When land was divided up, this was started from the tops of two facing hills: Martins Hill at Bromley and this other hill where St. Mary's was built; on reaching the valley floor it was found that distances had been miscalculated, leaving much smaller and cramped remaining portions at the bottom, the short-lands. However, we have not found proof of this attractive legend.

52. Canon H.F. Wolley spent his entire priesthood at St. Mary's Shortlands, a span of forty-five years. At its construction in 1867-68 he was a young curate-in-charge, and from the finished building's consecration in 1870 he was made vicar, when still aged only thirty-one. In 1902 he became an Honorary Canon of Canterbury. St. Mary's was originally almost alone on a hilltop, but for a few large expensive houses, but its successor is surrounded by suburbia. Sadly the old church was first damaged by a wartime landmine and then utterly ruined by a 1944 flying bomb, seen by parishioners to glide low over Shortlands onto this target. People who were children in the late Forties can boast of climbing up its steeple, or even jumping right over it; the secret was that it lay for some years, almost intact, on the ground where it had fallen.

Ye Olde Beckenham Curio Shoppe.

53. Old Beckenham was so picturesque that one could weep when walking its modern sterile High Street; though the road itself still twists like the country lane it once was. In this picture the date 1547 is visible, plus the newer date of 1902. Between the buildings is the sign of Beckenham Wheel Works, much in demand when travel was mainly by carriage or cart and cars were a novelty. At its lowest point this road is inclined to flooding, and boats have been rowed within modern memory. In 1878 water touched the tops of shop counters and stock floated out through the doors. Beckenham's doom as a village was sealed by the first railway in 1857, initially as a terminus. New trade and new residents came in, once city commuting was possible, principally of the wealthier type, creating its still surviving air of exclusivity.

The Fountain, Croydon Road Recreation Ground, Beckenham.

54. Croydon Road Recreation Ground, Beckenham, at some uncertain date, looking somewhat cluttered. Between the world wars the giant Beckenham Flower Show was sometimes held here, in massive marquees that drew almost Chelsea-sized crowds. The floral displays were most spectacular, and complemented by such attractions as swings, roundabouts, and miniature steam trains. As far back as the 1860s Beckenham prided itself on its flower shows, then held in the Rectory gardens, where a 'new and spacious' marquee was erected. Some of the displays were exotic, like Mr. Barry's grapes; others showed gardening for humbler folk: the 'jobbing gardeners' section for potatoes, cabbages, a peck of peas, cucumbers or beans.

MILITARY QUARTERS, KELSEY PARK, BECKENHAM. 2.   W. J. STEED, BECKENHAM.

55. Few Kentish mansions looked as extravagantly stately as did Kelsey at Beckenham, a flamboyant Scottish Baronial pile which was actually a clever re-facing of an older house. It was kept suitably ivy-grown and surrounded by impeccable grounds; it even had its own chapel. Kelsey as an ancient manor dated from either the 13th or 15th century, and was last privately owned by the rich banker Charles Hoare. When it came on the market Thornton, the local newspaper proprietor, led a campaign to have it purchased for the borough, and in 1911 the gigantic house was bought for only £13,511; two years later the grounds opened as **Kelsey Park**, but the house fell upon less happy times. During the Great War it became army quarters, though outwardly keeping its romantic appearance — as in this picture — but was then allowed to decay. It was demolished in 1921.

56. The placename 'Broom' crops up again, in unbelievably rural Broom Hill at Orpington, taken in the early 20th century. A mere sixty-odd years ago much of this most suburbanised of suburbs looked like this. Travel on deserted lanes was mainly under horsepower; yet the name of Orpington was about to enter early motoring history in a distinguished and now rare car called simply The Orpington. Developed by two bicycle repairers who turned to motor engineering, it began leaving the workshop in 1920. But only about a dozen were ever made, as new mass production forced them out of the commercial race. The Orpington slipped quietly into the annals of Kentish transport history.

57. Those comedians who unkindly joke about Orpington as the epitome of suburbia would scarcely believe that its traffic was once limited to a single pony cart parked outside a country house like this. Yet Orpington was an ancient settlement, and even now old fragments come to light. In about 1976 when some shops were demolished for redevelopment, an adjoining shop was discovered (or, rather, rediscovered) to have been adapted from a fine old coach-house belonging to a long lost estate whose grounds had occupied much of the present High Street site.

58. Chelsfield's peace is here broken only by one antique car. The lamp-post looks equally venerable. In Victorian times it was a popular country retreat for Sunday School and works outings, which were taken locally rather than by train to the coast. An account from 1883, as an example, describes an August Bank Holiday treat for the village children, when two hundred pupils plus hundreds of mothers, fathers and friends, sat down to a monster 'bun-fight' tea after playing at simple games and races. Sometimes such events culminated in the children's prize-giving ceremony, when good moral books were awarded for the three standard virtues of 'good conduct, diligence, and regular attendance'.

59. Green Street Green is here seen as it looked in 1902. Cyclists in particular favoured it, as a meeting point, as did ramblers bound for the North Downs. But in place of this charming scene there is now only a roundabout on the busy A21 road. However, the pretty Rose And Crown was spared, carefully pulled down and rebuilt on another site; in olden days, stagecoaches changed horses there. Green Street Green developed mainly after 1836, when the massive Oak Brewery opened; thereafter many residents worked there, and it was the focal point of local life until its closure in 1909, described by many as a tragedy. Its buildings were derelict until adapted as barracks in the Great War, and for plastics manufacture during the 1939-1945 conflict; it has also been used for private work.

60. The 'Golden Arrow' was one of Britain's most glamorous trains, ferrying the rich and famous to the Kent ports for onward passage to Paris. The sight of the Pullman cars behind one of the Southern's crack locomotives, kept in special condition for this run, never palled. Every day, people gathered on such viewpoints as the three footbridges between Shortlands and Bromley South to watch the train rush past. Apart from wartime interruptions, the 'Arrow' ran for forty-three years, until air travel destroyed its monopoly of fast travel to France. The farewell journeys were made in about 1972; but some of the magnificent Pullmans have been restored for the revived 'Orient Express'. This picture shows the 'Golden Arrow' on a spur between Bickley Junction and Orpington in June 1930, hauled by 'Lord Nelson' class 4-6-0 locomotive number 864.

61. Bickley has been described as 'the nobs' end of Bromley': a district of big and expensive Victorian properties and minor mansions, wearing an aura of wealth. Even now, some very pricey houses exist there. Here is shown a typical quiet road of genteel residences in 1907, deserted but for some road-sweepers, posing near the heavy gates of two large houses in wooded gardens. Historically as well as pictorially this is a crossroads, where old gentility and new suburbia overlap: in the background neat new pavements flank a smooth road, while in the foreground neither is properly developed and the road is rutted by cart-wheels.

CHISLEHURST VILLAGE.

March 17th 1904

62. Today Chislehurst is an unusual blend of suburb and country, with the country managing to hold its own. Its aspect may not be so wholly rural as in this pretty scene dated 1904 (even off the main thoroughfares, residents can hardly dawdle in the middle of the road like these relaxed villagers); but it still keeps some rural charm. Apart from the widespread commons, country hikes can be started within a quarter-mile south-east of Chislehurst station, where woods, sloping fields and running streams make London seem a hundred miles away, instead of only about ten. The past is everywhere about you, even on the busy road over the Common; where else in Greater London can one find such a sinister site marker as 'Hereabouts stood a gibbet'?

63. Chislehurst Water Tower was both picturesque and unusual, completely closing the top of steep Summer Hill. All traffic had to negotiate the narrow mediaeval style needle's eye arch; a very difficult feat for drivers of Number 227 buses, which edged through with only a few inches to spare. The tower was built by George Wythes as a combined grand entrance and water storage for his elaborate Bickley estate, and he intended to give it massive gates (which were never added). The monster tank across the top reputedly held up to 200,000 gallons of water taken from the many local springs. Inevitably, modern traffic increases spelled doom to this unique landmark; specially ironically, its demolition began on a Friday the thirteenth, in about 1963. One of Wythes' carved coats of arms was rescued to become part of a public seat commemorating the site of this lost Victorian heritage.

64. Locks Bottom, as a modern community, has built up the same close-knit spirit of its village days, as captured in this view from the 1920s. In particular it prides itself on a wonderland of Christmas lights, good enough to lure shoppers away from the bigger centres. The entire neo-Tudor parade is massed with lights, which continue through the old trees right up to the Farnborough main road.

65. Farnborough is still a favourite hikers' rendez-vous. Before family motoring, it was also popular with local employers for staging annual staff outings, based on such simple pleasures as games and sports in the field behind the church, and tea in the village. London costermongers broke their Bank Holiday trips by horse bus or char-à-banc to dance the knees-up outside the George to music by accordions and fiddles, sometimes following a previous stop outside the Beech Tree at Bromley, where their dancing and singing in the presence of their Pearly Kings attracted many spectators. Until recently red London buses terminated in the little square; earlier, this was an important staging post on the Hastings road and the George was a busy coaching inn.

66. The New Inn, Farnborough, seen in the 1920s (centre), enjoyed a strange moment of more modern fame, when in 1973 it had three names in one day. It started as the original New Inn; was renamed briefly as The Golden Nugget to complement a village Wild West Day; and then was officially renamed The Change Of Horses in recognition of its days as a staging post on the Old Kent Road run to Sevenoaks. These coaches deposited passengers overnight at the ancient White Lion at Locks Bottom, after which the coach and horses went ahead to be stabled behind the New Inn, where is now a car park. The coachman and his boy were probably also accommodated, perhaps in the loft over the stables. Gipsies used to barter outside the New Inn, especially in horse sales, the animals being trotted down the High Street to show their paces to buyers.

67. Even now Downe remains very rural, though part of a London Borough. This old view of the former Post Office, probably dating from the early 20th century, shows the main road rough and scarcely fit for traffic. The age of radio and TV would seem almost alien to such a retreat; yet Downe at about this period played a small part in radio development. At West Hill, near Darwin's old home, were once several tall thin pylons, anchored by a network of wires; they corresponded to a similar set near Elmers End. Between these two points Marconi and the Beckenham electrical pioneer Muirhead are believed to have experimented with link-ups to test the theory of transmission across country without connecting wires: hence the term wireless. Briefly a commemorative plaque was nailed to a tree nearby, but it was soon stolen.

68. Sleepy Downe, when its main road junction was still roughly made. At left is the Village Hall, used for dances and amateur dramatics, facing the majestic central feature known simply as The Tree. Darwin, Downe's most famous resident, lived nearby at Down or Downe House, renewed in the 18th century, and added a west wing for his large scientific library; in the study he wrote many major treatises. Darwin was described by one visitor, in a Bromley newspaper: 'A tall and venerable figure, with the broad shoulders of an Atlas supporting a world of thought.' In a famous local experiment begun in 1842, chalk was laid on the surface of a field and left undisturbed; thirty years later it had sunk, by the action of worms, seven inches down. Thus was explained why old relics are often discovered deeply buried.

69. Apart from one distant car, Downe in 1927 is deserted. In fact, it had changed little during the past half-century: a village where the simplest local event was news. To typify this aspect we look back to the time of the Penny Readings, given in the school room at an admission charge of one old penny. These sessions included, as well as readings from English literature and poetry, a selection of songs, glees and solos, intended to elevate the minds of countryfolk. The Reading reported in February 1869 was specially interesting for the entry: 'Mrs. Darwin kindly presided at the pianoforte, and accompanied the various songs with much ability. It is impossible to speak too highly of this lady's kindness, she having on all occasions evinced a most lively interest in these village entertainments.'

28   HAYES VILLAGE and POST OFFICE

70. Suburban Hayes bears little resemblance to this view in about 1908, where the only traffic is one horse and cart: an idyllic retreat until the mock-Tudor terrace builders laid hands on it. The most eminent village family were the political Pitts, of Hayes Place, whose estate has been completely built over. Pitt, the great Lord Chatham, was given a funeral in Westminster Abbey, but the ceremonial banners carried that day were later brought to Hayes church, to be kept for about seventy years. Then they disappeared, supposedly because an enthusiastic but unknowledgeable woman cleaner threw them away as grubby old rags, unworthy of her clean and tidy church. In 1920 a Hayes benefactress gave a new banner based on pictures of the original, which was placed over the chancel screen.

71. Unhappily, the pretty natural pond in this picture, once glowing with yellow irises, was filled in a few years ago, but at least the wild snowdrops still flourish in the churchyard of St. John's, West Wickham. About twenty years ago congregations at Evensong swelled so much that the vestry was taken for extra pews, and a new upstairs vestry and other rooms were discreetly added on the north side: to the right when looking from this viewpoint dated 1908. But today, as in almost all other churches, evening worshippers have dwindled, not least due to the lure of TV. West Wickham was overwhelmed by suburb builders in the thirties: no longer the 'pretty little village' of the late 19th century. The houses swept within one field of this ancient church and then halted, as miraculously as a tide kept back in a biblical drama. Its churchyard is still a most peaceful place.

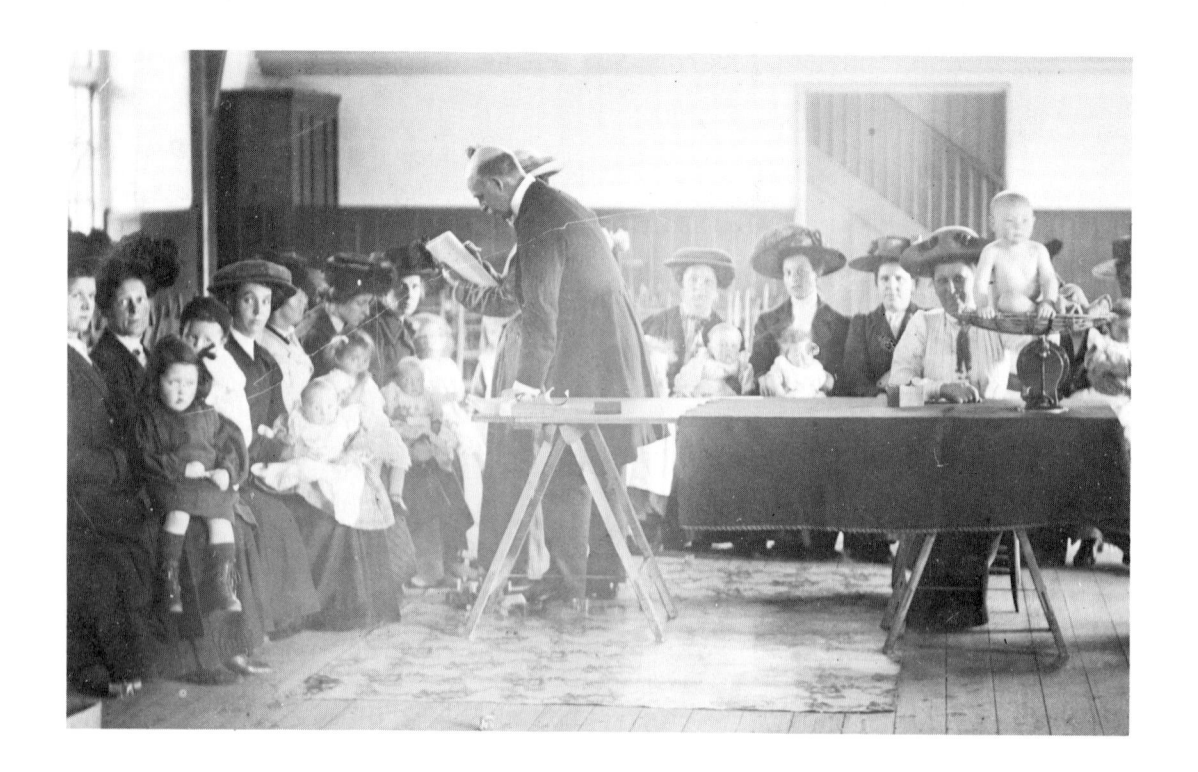

72. Before the National Health, young mothers took their babies weekly to the Infant Welfare, or Baby Clinic. There, nurses charted their weight and advised on upbringing, diet and minor ailments. The doctor, because he charged up to 3s.6d (17½p) a visit, was only called in real emergency. This Baby Clinic was pictured in 1912 at Bromley. The mothers are noticeably older than today's average age group. The setting is probably a church or school hall.

73. At the boundary extremity, where Bromley meets London SE6 and SE12, lies the huge residential area of Downham: a massive conception in town planning in the 1920s and 1930s that turned several miles of countryside into a New Town for Londoners. Today the thousands of cottage-style houses have mellowed into a certain attractiveness; but when this picture was taken in 1925, they were unimaginable. Downham Fields was then used by light aircraft, like the one here coming in to land, taking local people up on pleasure 'flips' for half-a-crown (12½p). Crowds line the field, as far as the eye can see, to gaze at the little planes. Early cowboy movies were shot on these hills, doing duty as the Wild West prairie for a small local studio.

74. Penge Empire died when TV arrived. Pleasant variety shows to a live orchestra no longer drew the crowd 'twice nightly'. Like other fading music halls it briefly became a cinema (The Essoldo) but has now vanished without trace. Into the 1950s it still staged variety and a Christmas pantomime, but its heyday was over. Yet, ironically, it had survived the war, defiantly continuing with a programme footnote: 'If an air raid warning be received during the performance the audience will be informed... Those desiring to leave the theatre may do so, but the performance will continue.' Most people sat tight. Admission prices then, much the same as in the Thirties, were: boxes 14s. and 10s (70p and 50p), stalls 2s.3d (11p), circle 1s.9d (9p), pit 1s.3d (6p) and the gods (or 'up on the shelf') only 8d (3½p).

15199 BECKENHAM ROAD AVENUE.   PENGE.

75. Where is or was Beckenham Road Avenue at Penge? We cannot find it under that name on modern maps. Nevertheless, it typifies the half-country, half-town character of the area in Victorian and Edwardian times: a genteel haven for bankers, businessmen and shop owners until it petered out into the smaller and cheaper streets of Penge proper. 'Since the opening of the railway the rateable value of the property in Beckenham had increased very rapidly, and now it reached the sum of £72,373,' reported one paper in 1873, which added: 'In 1871 the population was 6090; the house property was estimated at a million; and the area of the parish was 2881 acres.' By then Beckenham comprised four burgeoning residential areas: Beckenham with New Beckenham; Laurie Park; Shortlands; and Elmers End, all of which were developed even more intensively in the next century.

76. Everything about 'Screaming Alice' – the Crystal Palace – was larger than life, including the manner of its passing. In November 1936 it ended as one of the biggest fires in London or Kent history, burning from end to end; glass panes, blown upwards by hot air, flew across rooftops to crash in neighbouring gardens. Half Bromley gathered on Martins Hill to watch this awesome sight; the collapse of the great central transept was heard as the roar of a battle. A Bromley member of an orchestra rehearsing that night told how the fleeing players heard deep gruesome groans from the huge organ, as furnace air entered its pipes. Thursday in Bromley was not only market day; it was also Crystal Palace firework night. So amazing were the displays that even from this distance they were worth watching.